GROWING YOUR OWN GARDEN

by Rebecca E. Hirsch

CHERRY LAKE PUBLISHING • ANN ARBOR, MICHIGAN

Published in the United States of America
by Cherry Lake Publishing
Ann Arbor, Michigan
www.cherrylakepublishing.com

Printed in the United States of America
Corporate Graphics Inc
January 2010
CLSP06

Consultants: Karen O'Connor, co-owner, Mother Earth Gardens, Minneapolis, Minnesota;
Gail Saunders-Smith, associate professor of literacy, Beeghly College of Education,
Youngstown State University

Editorial direction: Book design and illustration:
Amy Van Zee   Emily Love

Photo credits: Anthony Harris/Shutterstock Images, cover, 1; Denis and Yulia Pogostins/
Shutterstock Images, 5; Mona Makela/iStockphoto, 6; Fotolia, 9; LianeM/Shutterstock
Images, 11; Sally Scott/Shutterstock Images, 13; Shutterstock Images, 14, 19, 25; Rich
Legg/iStockphoto, 17; Chepko Danil Vitalevich/Shutterstock Images, 20; Elena Moiseeva/
Shutterstock Images, 23; Tereza Dvorak/Shutterstock Images, 27

Library of Congress Cataloging-in-Publication Data
Hirsch, Rebecca E.
 Save the planet : growing your own garden / by Rebecca Hirsch.
   p. cm. — (Language arts explorer)
 ISBN 978-1-60279-657-7 (hardback) — ISBN 978-1-60279-666-9 (pbk.)
 1. Vegetable gardening—Juvenile literature. I. Title. II. Series.

SB324.H57 2010
635—dc22

2009038093

**Cherry Lake Publishing would like to acknowledge the work of The Partnership for 21st
Century Skills. Please visit www.21centuryskills.org for more information.**

TABLE OF CONTENTS

You are being given a mission. The facts in What You Know will help you accomplish it. Remember What You Know while you are reading the story. The story will help you answer the questions at the end of the book. Have fun on this adventure!

YOUR MISSION

Your mission is to investigate how food is grown in a garden. How do people grow their own food? What kind of work is needed to grow food? Why would people grow food when they can buy it from the store? Remember to keep What You Know in mind.

WHAT YOU KNOW

★ Every place on Earth has its own weather pattern. Weather varies from place to place.

★ Plants grow in different ways. Some plants grow quickly. Others grow slowly. Some are tall, and some are short. Some plants grow well in cool weather and some in hot weather.

★ Different plant parts have different jobs. The seed contains a new plant that grows when the seed gets water and sunshine. Roots anchor the plant in the ground and suck up water. Leaves turn sunshine into food for the plant.

Now you're ready to get out into the garden. Read the following journal about the growing of a garden.

Growing a garden takes a lot of work, but it is rewarding to grow your own food!

Today our teacher made an announcement. She said our school would grow a garden this spring. Then she gave us more news. She told us that our class will be in charge of the garden! We will plant seeds and take care of the plants. At the end of the school year, we will host a harvest party and invite the whole school.

Planning Ahead

We began working on our garden right away. It was too cold to work outside, but we could work inside. Our teacher said the first step is to decide what seeds to plant. She

Seeds come in many shapes and sizes.

GARDENS AND WEATHER

Gardeners must keep in mind the climate where they live. A garden in Florida will be different from one in Minnesota. A Florida gardener might start growing vegetables in winter. A gardener in Minnesota will wait until spring or summer before beginning to plant. Sometimes, a Minnesota gardener might start the seeds in a pot indoors. Then, the gardener can plant the seedlings in the ground when the weather gets warmer.

handed out seed catalogs. They were filled with pictures of vegetables and flowers. Our teacher gave us two rules to follow for choosing plants. The first is to choose plants that grow well in our climate, or weather pattern. She said different plants grow well in different places, depending on the weather. The second rule is to plant what we like to eat, because we will eat what we grow.

We looked at the catalogs for a long time. Our teacher showed us plants that grow well in our home state, Pennsylvania. We found some plants that will grow well in the cool weather of spring and some that grow well in the heat of summer. We decided to grow some plants to eat. We also wanted to plant something that would bring birds to the garden. Finally, we made our list of what to grow. Our garden will have peas, lettuce, carrots, corn, pumpkins, and sunflowers. We will eat the vegetables, and the sunflowers will be for birds to eat. ★

Today we put on our coats and walked outside. It was cold and windy. Our teacher showed us the spot where our garden will be. Right now it looks like a large square of dirt in the middle of the schoolyard. We walked around the garden and made plans. We decided to grow sunflowers in one corner and pumpkins in another. We will grow corn along the opposite side. In the middle we will grow carrots, peas, and lettuce.

It is too cold to work in the garden. Our teacher told us there is something we can do indoors. We went back into the classroom. She passed out graph paper. We made maps showing our garden plan. She said smart gardeners always have a plan before they start. It is important to make sure

GARDEN LOCATION

A good place for a garden is somewhere you can see every day. A garden that is out of the way is easy to forget. Also, a garden should be located away from trees. Most vegetables need plenty of sunshine. They also need room for their roots to grow away from the roots of large trees.

Gardeners must plan before they begin their gardens.

each plant gets enough sun. Sometimes tall plants prevent the sun from getting to shorter plants, so gardeners have to plan which plant goes where. ★

A warm breeze was blowing today. It felt like spring was on the way. We walked outside. A man who is an expert gardener was waiting for us in the garden. He showed us a pile of black soil that had been dumped in the middle of the garden. He called it compost.

What Is Compost?

The gardener said compost is made from remains of plant material, like leaves and grass clippings, mixed with food scraps. When the leaves, clippings, apple cores, eggshells, and coffee grounds are mixed together, they rot and turn into compost. We were surprised. The black soil didn't look like or smell like it was made of rotting food.

MAKING COMPOST

Many gardeners make compost for their gardens. Instead of becoming garbage, food scraps, grass clippings, and fall leaves are recycled back into the earth. Compost is good for the environment because it reduces the amount of garbage people throw away. It provides natural, healthy soil for plants.

Compost is made of plant material and some types of food scraps.

The man told us that compost helps plants grow big and healthy. It acts as a fertilizer by giving plants the nutrients they need to grow. The plant materials in the compost nourish the new plants. Compost also holds water like a sponge, so plants get water even when there has been no rain.

First, we spread the pile of compost all over the garden. Then, we used shovels to mix the compost into the soil. Finally, we raked the soil until it was smooth and flat. It was a lot of work, but now our soil is ready. The next step will be to plant our seeds. ★

Planting day is finally here! We took our packets of seeds and ran to the garden. Our teacher handed out trowels, which are small shovels you hold in one hand. We used the trowels to dig shallow rows in the soil. We sprinkled tiny carrot seeds in each row. Then we covered the seeds with a thin layer of soil and patted it down. Next, we made more rows and planted tiny lettuce seeds. Finally, we planted pea seeds, which were bigger and looked like shriveled-up peas. Instead of a straight row, we planted the peas in a circle. We did this because peas are climbing plants. They need something sturdy to climb on, so we will build a trellis.

COOL-WEATHER PLANTS

Some plants grow best in cool weather. Carrots, lettuce, and peas are plants that thrive in cooler weather. They can survive if the temperature goes below freezing. They can even survive if snow covers them. This is helpful if there is unusually cold weather in the spring!

Building a Trellis

We all worked together to make the trellis. It was shaped like a teepee and was made of long bamboo poles that were tied together at the top with string. We wound more string around the teepee, weaving it over and under the bamboo poles.

After everything was planted and the trellis was built, we watered the garden. Our teacher told us that new plants need a lot of water so their roots can grow well. We will water often and check the seeds every day. We are excited to see them grow! ★

Some plants grow onto trellises.
The trellis supports the plant.

The past few days have been drizzly and wet. But today, the sun came out and the ground dried. It felt good to step into the warm sunshine.

When we got to the garden, we didn't notice anything different at first. Then we looked closely and saw that tiny lettuce plants were growing!

The pea plants had also pushed their way out of the ground. They had even begun climbing the trellis. We could see tendrils that looked like thin green threads growing out of the plants. The tendrils were curling themselves around the strings of the trellis.

We tried to find our carrot plants but couldn't see any. We thought something was wrong, but our teacher said not

Plants need plenty of water and sunshine to grow.

CARING FOR THE PLANET

Most gardeners care about Earth. They believe in being careful with its resources. One way gardeners can protect those resources is by conserving water. Many gardeners use rain barrels to conserve water.

to worry. She said some plants, such as lettuce and peas, start growing right away. Others take longer. She said that if we make sure they are moist every day, soon our carrots would grow.

We watered the plants with water from a rain barrel. The rain barrel collects rainwater from the roof of the school. Water pours from a downspout off the roof and into the barrel on the ground. The water that collects does not contain chemicals, so it is good for watering plants.

Our teacher said that morning and evening are the best times to water. She said that in the morning and evening, the air is cool. Water that is sprayed or poured on the garden soaks into the ground. The water reaches the plant roots, where the plants soak it up and use it to grow.

In the afternoon, the air is warm. Water that lands on the ground can evaporate. Warmed by the sun, the water turns into vapor and goes into the air. Water that evaporates doesn't get to the plants that need it. The water is wasted. That is why smart gardeners know to water in the morning or evening. ★

Today, we went outside to work in the garden. It was warm. The sky was blue with puffy clouds. Each time we come to the garden, the plants seem a little bigger. The peas have climbed halfway up the trellis. The carrots are tiny but growing. Carrots grow underground, but we can see the green, frilly tops poking out of the ground.

Our plants aren't the only things growing in the garden. So are weeds. Our teacher says the weeds must be pulled out. Plants that are surrounded by weeds won't grow well.

We began pulling weeds. Every weed had to be pulled out, root and all. Some weeds slid right out of the ground.

WEEDS

A weed is any plant that grows where it is not wanted. Weeds are bad for gardens. They crowd and smother garden plants. They take up root space, so the plants the gardener wants cannot grow as well. Weeds steal water and sunshine. It is important to pull them out. Because they can come back, it is important to weed often.

When weeding, it is important to pull out the weed's root.

Other times the weed snapped in half and the root stayed in the soil. Our teacher said if the root was left in the ground, the weed would just keep coming back again. So after a while, we decided to use trowels to dig out the weeds. Weeding is hard work, but we all agreed our garden looked much better afterward. We knew our plants would grow better, too. ★

This morning we looked at the garden. No rain has fallen for a week. The soil felt hard and dry. Some of the carrots looked wilted. Their stems and leaves drooped. Without water it looked like our plants might die.

Our teacher said that growing plants need about one inch (2.54 cm) of water each week. It is best to give each plant a long watering. This way, the water will go deep into the soil, and the roots will follow the water. Then the plants will have strong, deep roots.

To test how much water we gave the plants, we put a dish beside the plants. We watered and watered. Then we used a ruler and measured how much water had landed in the dish. It was only half an inch (1.27 cm).

WATERING FREQUENCY

Growing plants need to be watered weekly. One way to tell if a garden needs water is to check the soil. Poke a finger deep into the soil. How does it feel? If it is dry, it is time to give your plants a good, long drink.

New plants need a lot of water so their roots can grow strong.

So we watered and watered some more. Finally we had given the plants an inch of water. There were shiny mud puddles all over the garden. ★

Today was another warm day for working in the garden. All week the weather has been warm. Our plants have grown big. The lettuce plants are as big as basketballs! The peas have climbed to the top of the trellis!

It is time to plant the corn, pumpkins, and sunflowers. These are the plants that need warm weather. We had to wait until now because these plants will die if there is a

Some plants, such as corn, need warm weather to grow.

frost. Where we live in Pennsylvania, it is now safe for warm-weather plants. Frosts are usually over by this time in May. People who live in colder areas may need to wait longer.

The first thing we planted was the corn. We dug rows in the soil. Then we dropped in corn seeds, one by one. Next, we planted pumpkin seeds in one corner. Pumpkins grow on long vines that spread across the ground. They need lots of room and lots of time to grow. Our teacher said the pumpkins wouldn't be ready until fall. Finally, we planted sunflower seeds. The sunflowers will make our garden look nice. They will also bring birds that will come to the garden to eat the sunflower seeds. ★

BIODIVERSITY

Many gardens attract insects and birds. Bees collect pollen from the flowers. Then they bring the pollen to other flowers. This is how flowers reproduce. Birds eat insects. This keeps pests under control. Gardens can increase biodiversity, or the variety of living things in one place.

The corn, sunflowers, and pumpkins have poked out of the soil. Finally, everything is growing! The new plants are still small. Our teacher says they will grow a lot in the heat of summer.

Today was our first chance to eat what we've been growing. We tasted different vegetables to see if we liked them. First, we tasted a few tender lettuce leaves. Then we snapped pea pods off the vine. We ate the pods whole. They tasted crisp and sweet. Next, we dug carrots out of the ground using trowels. We rinsed off the dirt and took a bite. The carrots were small, like the baby carrots in the

EATING FRESH

Fruits and vegetables at the grocery store may have been picked weeks before reaching the store. This means they were not ripe when they were picked. Foods that are picked before they are ripe do not have the full flavor or nutrients found in ripe food. Food from a garden tastes better because it is fresh. Growing your own food has another benefit: It saves fuel because the food hasn't been trucked or flown in from far away.

Carrots grow underground.

store, but much sweeter. The carrots were crunchy, too. Our teacher said the carrots we left in the ground will grow.

We were surprised at how fresh everything tasted. All the vegetables tasted better than ones from a store. We decided that food tastes best when you grow it yourself! ★

Today the sun was shining, and the air was warm. It was perfect weather for a harvest party! When school began, we prepared for the party. Our teacher handed out big bowls, and we headed to the garden. We filled the bowls with peas, carrots, and big heads of lettuce. Then we went back to the classroom. We rinsed all the vegetables. We put some of the pea pods and carrots in a bowl and had ranch dressing for dipping. We mixed a big salad using the cut-up lettuce, carrots, and peas.

Homegrown Food

We brought the food outside. Tables were set up near the garden. All the other classes came to the party, too. Each class brought food to share, but ours was the only food

PESTICIDES

It is important to rinse the fruits and vegetables you buy from the store with water before you eat them. Some farmers use pesticides, which are chemicals that keep away insects that could destroy the crops. In large amounts, these pesticides can be harmful to humans. Also, soil contains germs. Rinsing your food can help keep you healthy!

Fresh vegetables taste great!

that was homegrown. The food from our garden was a big hit. Everyone thought it tasted great.

The harvest party was a lot of fun. It was great to eat food we grew ourselves and share it with the other kids. Growing a garden was a lot of work, but it was fun, too. We learned a lot about how to care for the earth. We also learned that taking care of the earth can taste delicious. We can't wait to see how the corn, pumpkins, and sunflowers grow! ★

MISSION ACCOMPLISHED!

Congratulations! You have learned a lot about how to grow food. You've learned that gardeners should choose plants that they like and that grow well in their climate. Many gardeners also choose plants that help birds and insects. You have learned many ways that people help plants grow. They add compost and water and they pull weeds. You have discovered some of the benefits of gardens. Gardens help save money and fuel. They give food to birds, insects, and people. They teach people how to care for the earth. Congratulations on a mission well done.

CONSIDER THIS

Consider the benefits of growing your own garden. By asking yourself more questions about gardening, you might just start a mission of your own!

★ What are some things to consider when planning a garden? Why are these things important?
★ Can you think of other ways in which gardens help animals? How do birds and insects help gardens?

Many vegetables can be grown in gardens.

★ What are some of the benefits of homegrown food?

★ How could growing your own food help you save money?

★ Where might you grow a garden? What types of plants would you grow?

GLOSSARY

biodiversity (bye-oh-duh-VURS-it-ee) the number and variety of living things in one place

climate (KLYE-mit) the regular pattern of weather in a certain place

compost (KOM-pohst) a decaying mixture of leaves, grass clippings, food scraps, and manure used to enrich the soil

conserve (kuhn-SURV) to use something carefully to keep it from being lost or wasted

evaporate (i-VAP-uh-rate) to change from a liquid into a vapor that rises into the air

fertilizer (FUR-tuh-lize-ur) a natural or artificial substance added to soil to help plants grow

nutrient (NOO-tree-uhnt) a mineral or a chemical needed by a living thing to stay healthy

pod (POD) a casing that holds the seeds of a plant

pollen (POL-uhn) a powdery dust spread from flower to flower, allowing the plants to reproduce

rain barrel (RAYN ba-ruhl) a barrel or tank that is used to collect and store rainwater

resources (REE-sorss-ez) valuable things found on Earth, such as water and trees

tendril (TEN-drill) a thin, coiling stem that a plant uses to climb a trellis

thrive (THRIVE) to do well

trellis (TREL-iss) a frame made to support climbing plants

wilted (WILT-ed) limp and drooping from lack of water

BOOKS

Bull, Jane. *The Gardening Book*. New York, NY:
DK Publishing, 2003.

Spohn, Rebecca. *Ready, Set, Grow! A Kids' Guide to Gardening*. Tucson, AZ: Good Year Books, 2007.

WEB SITES

University of Illinois Extension "My First Garden"

http://urbanext.illinois.edu/firstgarden/

Learn how to find the best spot for a garden, plan your garden, and see pictures of other kids' gardens at this site.

Texas A&M University's "Composting for Kids"

http://aggie-horticulture.tamu.edu/sustainable/slidesets/kidscompost/cover.html

This site contains a helpful slide show demonstrating how to create and use a compost pile.

MAKE A GARDEN JOURNAL

Make a garden or nature journal. Use a blank notebook or make your own following one of the designs on this Web site: http://www.makingbooks.com/freeprojects.shtml. Take your journal outside to a special place such as a garden, your backyard, your schoolyard, or a park. Draw or write about your favorite things that grow and live there.

WATCH SEEDS GROW

Moisten a paper towel with water and then wring it out. Lay the paper towel flat and sprinkle some seeds on it. Try dried beans, sunflower seeds, apple seeds, or any other kind of seed you like. Roll up the paper towel with the seeds inside. Put the whole thing into a plastic bag or a jar with a lid. Keep the bag or jar closed so the paper towel stays moist. Every day or two, unroll the paper towel to check the progress of your seeds. Before long you should see a tiny plant growing. If you want to keep growing the plant, fill a pot with soil and tuck the roots of the young plant into the soil. Add water when the soil is dry. Put the seedling by a sunny window or under grow lights.

INDEX

ABOUT THE AUTHOR

Rebecca E. Hirsch, PhD, writes books about science and the environment for children. A former molecular biologist, she writes from her home in State College, Pennsylvania, where she lives with her husband and three children.

ABOUT THE CONSULTANTS

Karen O'Connor is a gardening and local food advocate from Minnesota. She is co-owner of Mother Earth Gardens in Minneapolis, an independent garden center focusing on organic and sustainable gardening. She lives with her husband, two sons, and several small pets.

Gail Saunders-Smith is a former classroom teacher and Reading Recovery teacher leader. Currently she teaches literacy courses at Youngstown State University in Ohio. Gail is the author of many books for children and three professional books for teachers.